A Peaceful WORLD

Written by Alice Harman

Illustrated by David Broadbent

Franklin Watts
First published in Great Britain in 2019 by The Watts Publishing Group
Copyright © The Watts Publishing Group, 2019

Produced for Franklin Watts by
White-Thomson Publishing Ltd
www.wtpub.co.uk

ISBN (HB): 978 1 4451 6401 4
ISBN (PB): 978 1 4451 6402 1

Series Editor: Georgia Amson-Bradshaw
Series Designer: David Broadbent
All Illustrations by: David Broadbent
Consultant: Dr Synne L. Dyvik

Printed in Dubai

Franklin Watts
An imprint of
Hachette Children's Group
Part of The Watts Publishing Group
Carmelite House
50 Victoria Embankment
London EC4Y 0DZ

An Hachette UK Company
www.hachette.co.uk
www.franklinwatts.co.uk

Facts, figures and dates were correct when going to press.

CONTENTS

Look out for this little book symbol to find definitions of important words. Other definitions can be found in the glossary on page 30.

What is peace?

Peace means people getting along, with no wars or serious fighting. It doesn't mean that no one ever argues with each other – that's not realistic.

Living peacefully means finding ways to compromise and deal with disagreements in a calm, respectful way – without hurting and threatening each other.

Most people want a peaceful life, but peace can be hard to maintain. This is true on a global scale, too.

War and peace

In the last 3,400 years, there have only been 268 years in total where there have been no recorded wars – that means humans have been at war for 92 per cent of that time.

War can be officially defined as a conflict in which more than 1,000 people are killed, so 'peace' in this sense is just a time without these big conflicts. There were still arguments and fighting on a smaller scale.

Compromise

A type of agreement in which people who want different things decide to each give up or change part of what they want in order to stop the argument.

Fragile peace

Peace doesn't always last forever once it has been achieved. Arguments can start up and turn violent very quickly, so part of creating peace is putting systems in place that aim to make sure everything stays peaceful.

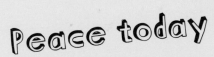

Peace today

Our world is generally much more peaceful today than it has been in the past, in terms of numbers killed in conflict. However, millions still die every year as a result of violence.

Peace is something that everyone has to work together to build, both in our own lives and communities and across the world.

What is conflict?

Conflict can mean anything from differences of opinion to full-scale war.

Everyone experiences conflict at some point, whether it is disagreements with family and friends, unpleasant tensions in the local community or across the country, or worries about terrorism and the possibility of war.

It can make us very anxious and upset and many people try to avoid conflict wherever possible.

Terrorism
The threat or use of violence, especially against civilians (people not in the armed forces), linked to a political or religious view.

Making history

Conflict plays a huge part in shaping history. War can mean countries win or lose land, split up or even disappear altogether. Forceful action against the government can change who is in power and what the country's future looks like.

Hate and violence against certain people, such as those of a particular ethnicity, religion, gender or sexual orientation, can seriously impact and even end their lives.

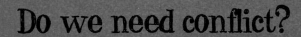

Do we need conflict?

Conflict isn't always a bad thing. For example, if someone is behaving cruelly or unfairly then they may not stop until someone else stands up to them and tells them they disagree with their behaviour.

But how we handle conflict is important. Is it acceptable to act violently towards someone who is behaving badly? To try and create a positive, peaceful world, we need to resolve conflicts sensitively and avoid future problems.

This is as true on a global scale as it is on a personal level. Conflict is sometimes necessary to reveal and stop injustices in a society, but it has to be handled carefully.

Why is peace important?

How do you feel when you are in the middle of an argument with someone? Relaxed? Happy? Able to focus on school and be kind to other people? Hmm, maybe not. More likely you feel distracted and worried and a bit snappy.

On a larger scale, the same thing happens with societies in conflict, especially when the conflict escalates into war. In wartime, fighting takes over as the top priority, bringing positive progress to a halt and very quickly making everything worse.

Effects of war

Schools close and children can't get an education; farms are destroyed and people don't have enough food; hospitals and basic services can't function and people become ill; law and order dissolves and many are victims of terrible crimes.

People lose their families, their homes, their jobs, their businesses, everything they have worked to achieve. They may become refugees and face terrible danger while trying to reach safety.

Deaths in war

And, of course, death is the very worst consequence of war and serious conflict. Every minute, someone in the world dies from armed violence.

In the twentieth century, it is thought that over 100 million people around the world died as a result of war. It is difficult, and frightening, to even imagine the human reality of these numbers.

Recovering from war

Keeping the peace is so important because of the devastation that war brings, and also because of how difficult it is to recover afterwards.

People have to live with the trauma of what happened to them and broken societies have to try and work together again. Everything that was destroyed has to be rebuilt when all the money has already been spent on war. In these conditions, conflict can soon start up again.

Refugee
A person forced to leave their country to escape danger and find safety in another place.

what causes conflict?

People argue about all sorts of things, from silly annoyances to very serious issues. There are so many reasons that it is impossible to list all of them, but often there are some key problems that can cause tension to explode into real fighting – on a personal and a global scale.

It's mine!

You have probably been in an argument with someone because you both want something and it seems like only one person can have it. On a larger scale, competition for land and natural resources, such as water or oil, can be a massive trigger for war.

No, my way!

You may have been in a situation where someone is trying to take over and get their own way. This battle for power, one group's desire to make everyone live by certain rules, is at the heart of many complicated conflicts.

My team!

People's loyalty to their group – whether it is their country, religion, political party or gang – can make them see their fellow humans simply as 'enemies' that they have to defeat. Ignorance, fear and hatred of different ways of living, as well as a history of past fighting between groups, can also tie into this and lead to violence.

Not so simple

A war can begin because of a complicated combination of all these reasons, or different ones altogether. It can sometimes be difficult to work out exactly why a conflict has started, especially for an outsider who doesn't know the culture or history of a particular place.

Think about the last three times you were involved in an argument. What caused the conflict each time? Try to think back to the very start of the problem. Write down the causes, as we will return to them in the activity on page 13.

Keeping the peace

Peace means listening, talking and compromising even when we think we're right and we feel angry and upset with others, in order to avoid a full-blown argument.

Good neighbours

Building peace can be effective on a local level as well as a global one. For example, in an area where a lot of people from different countries have recently moved in, friendly events such as street parties can help neighbours get to know each other and stop misunderstandings and bad feeling from building up.

United Nations (UN)

An organisation with many member countries that works for world peace and development.

World peace

The United Nations and many different charities and organisations around the world focus a lot of energy on keeping the peace by preventing conflict in the first place. They aim to help people understand each other and put agreements in place to try to avoid arguments and stop tensions rising any further.

From war to peace

Peacekeeping is also very important after a major conflict, when there is still a lot of hurt and anger and people may want to take revenge for what has happened.

Many countries have fallen back into violence and war within just a few years of a previous conflict. People have to learn, and be helped by outside forces where necessary, to live alongside each other peacefully.

Look back at your answer to the activity on page 11. How might you have prevented these arguments? Be creative with your methods – for example, if a sibling took something of yours without asking, maybe you could draw up a poster of house rules and agree forfeits for breaking them.

Working it out

Has a parent or teacher ever helped you make up with someone, even when you were angry and didn't want to? There are international organisations that work in a similar way to stop communities fighting and make peace. They often mediate between communities at war and write up peace agreements that both sides agree to and trust that the other will honour.

Mediate
To help people work through their conflict by leading talks between them and keeping things calm.

Peaceful solutions

When both sides agree to it, the UN can send in its peacekeeping soldiers to try and maintain order and protect civilians. The UN can also put sanctions in place to pressure a country to stop using violence against other countries or its own people.

Sanctions
Non-violent penalties, such as banning trade with a country, that aim to change that country's actions.

The mediation game

Try out this mediation game with your friends. Split into three groups: 1, 2 and 3. Each group comes up with three conflict scenarios, writes each one down on a piece of paper, then folds them and drops them all into a big bowl.

The referee (who could be a parent or teacher) reads out a scenario. Two people, one from Group 2 and one from Group 3, come forward to represent the two sides of the argument. A third person, from Group 1, comes up to act as the mediator between them.

The timer is set for five minutes. Each side has one minute to present their argument, then the mediator has three minutes to help both parties come to an agreement.

When the timer goes off, Groups 2 and 3 have two minutes to each decide a score out of ten for the mediator and hand it in to the referee. Repeat the game with mediators from each group in turn.

At the end, all the mediators' scores are added together for each group, and the group with the highest overall score wins.

An unfair fight

For peace to really exist, everyone has to be able to speak and be listened to. A situation may look peaceful if there is no shouting or violence, but if people are scared to share their views and ask for what they want, that is called oppression and it isn't the same as real peace. An unjust society is not a peaceful one.

Out of balance

You may have found already in your own life that in some conflicts both sides don't have the same amount of power. For example, if you have an argument with your parents, your teachers or your older siblings you may feel that they have an unfair advantage over you.

The same can be true on a national and international scale. If people protesting against unfair treatment by the government, police or powerful companies are ignored entirely or met with violence, what should they do?

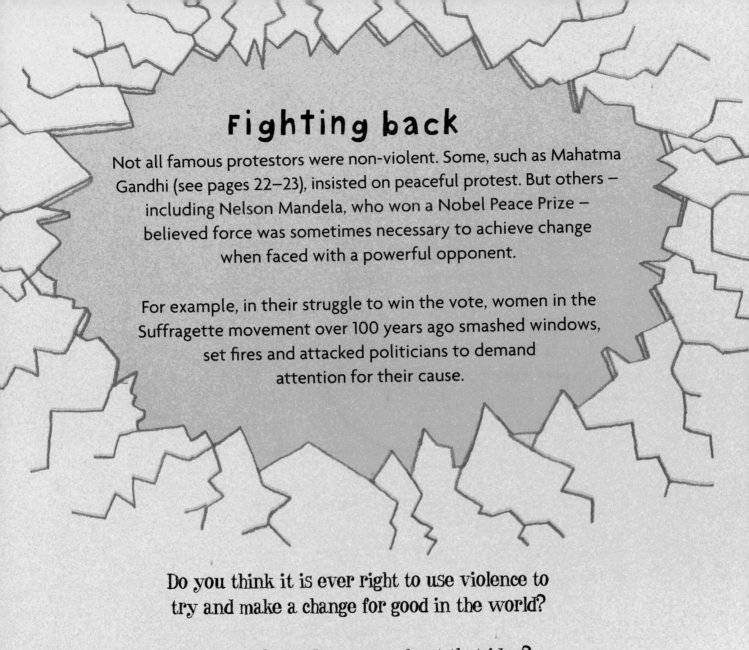

Fighting back

Not all famous protestors were non-violent. Some, such as Mahatma Gandhi (see pages 22–23), insisted on peaceful protest. But others – including Nelson Mandela, who won a Nobel Peace Prize – believed force was sometimes necessary to achieve change when faced with a powerful opponent.

For example, in their struggle to win the vote, women in the Suffragette movement over 100 years ago smashed windows, set fires and attacked politicians to demand attention for their cause.

Do you think it is ever right to use violence to try and make a change for good in the world?

What might be dangerous about that idea?

VOTES FOR WOMEN

CONSEQUENCES

As we have seen, the path to war or peace can be very complicated. In this activity, try to make decisions that will keep the peace.

Question 1
The country of Rafland has moved soldiers into part of a neighbouring country, Harka, and will not withdraw them. It says that the area is rightfully theirs as it was unfairly taken in a previous conflict. Should the UN enforce sanctions in Rafland?

NO →

Question 3
Rafland takes over the north of Harka. Its leaders will only agree to peace talks if Harka's violent nationalist resistance is declared a terrorist organisation by your country. Will you do this?

YES

NO

YES ↓

NO ↗

Question 2
Rafland is angry and accuses the UN of unfair treatment. It refuses to accept peacekeeping forces or mediation. Harka asks for weapons to protect itself from Rafland's larger army. Should other countries send weapons?

YES →

Question 4
Harka's government has been overthrown by nationalist rebels who are unhappy with its weak response to Rafland's invasion. They are armed with high-tech foreign weapons and are committing horrific violence. Should other countries help restore the government?

YES

NO

Outcome A
Rafland and Harka enter peace talks and the fighting ends; Rafland keeps the invaded territory. Harka's people are angry, and unrest between the government and nationalist rebels needs further peacekeeping.

Outcome B
The fighting continues for many years, with the border moving back and forth. People flee the area and settle as refugees elsewhere. Peace talks eventually end the conflict.

Outcome C
Rafland, alarmed by the rebels' violence, agrees to make peace with Harka's newly restored government and return some territory. Many in Harka resent the international meddling but there is some stability for now.

Outcome D
The rebels take over Harka and successfully fight off Rafland's invasion. The new regime rules by violence and although there is no war, many people are killed for disobeying the strict laws.

 How did you do?

Negotiating peace

Negotiating peace between countries or groups that are locked in a fierce conflict can be incredibly difficult. The negotiator has to try and understand both sides, remaining calm and fair while huge emotions rage and innocent civilians remain in life-or-death situations. It's a lot of pressure!

On several occasions the Nobel Peace Prize has been won by famous negotiators, such as Martti Ahtisaari, to recognise that their work has saved countless lives.

Negotiate

To come to an agreement with someone, or help others to do the same.

Challenge

In this activity it is your turn to act as a negotiator. There is a plan to develop an underused area in the local park, and the council has asked for suggestions from park users.

Two large groups of young people want different things: one group of 25 is desperate for a basketball court and another of 30 is equally set on a skateboard park. Some in each group have said that they would like to try the other sport.

Another separate group of eight older people have said they would like to plant a community herb garden in the area.

There is an indoor basketball court at a local gym five minutes away, but you have to pay to play there and the nearest skate park is a half-hour drive across town.

The skaters use a concrete area with benches near the front of the park to skate. Some of the basketball players have come there to talk to the skaters, and there have been arguments.

There have also been some nasty comments and threats on social media, and at school one girl had her phone smashed against the wall when she tried to take and puncture a boy's basketball.

Can you come up with a 'win-win' situation and a strategy for keeping the peace? Is there anyone else whose voice should be included?

Making change happen: Indian independence

The forced British rule of India lasted almost 100 years from 1858 to 1947. During this time, there was not much violent fighting but Indian people were oppressed and treated as second-class citizens in their own country.

Indian people struggled for decades to end British rule, with violent and non-violent action. In 1914, Mohandas Gandhi – known as Mahatma Gandhi – joined the fight for Indian independence. He was committed to using non-violent protest as a means to peacefully demand positive change.

Satyagraha

At the heart of Gandhi's philosophy, and of the peaceful Indian independence movement that he led, was the idea of *satyagraha*, a new term that Gandhi created from the Sanskrit words for 'truth' (satya) and 'polite firmness' (graha).

Satyagraha describes the special power of non-violent protest, of people behaving peacefully while they fight against evil. Because violence is never allowed, people must show their strength in other ways.

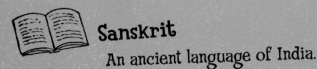

Sanskrit
An ancient language of India.

Peaceful tactics

Encouraged by Gandhi, millions of Indians did just that. They stopped buying British products, refused to pay taxes to the British government and took part in peaceful protests and marches.

One of the most famous events was the Salt March in 1930, in which thousands of people marched together for over 385 kilometres. Gandhi also brought worldwide attention to the cause by staging several protests in which he refused to eat for up to 21 days at a time.

Working together

One of the movement's greatest achievements was that so many supporters from India's different religions worked together peacefully for independence, despite the long history of conflict between them.

The united effort helped the protestors to win their long fight in 1947, when India gained independence and finally became free of British rule.

Profile: Leymah Gbowee

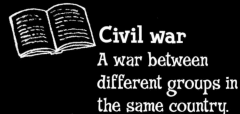

Civil war
A war between different groups in the same country.

Leymah Gbowee grew up dreaming of being a doctor but when she was just seventeen, a terrible civil war broke out in her country, Liberia, in West Africa. She has said that the war turned her 'from a child to an adult in a matter of hours'.

Towards the end of the war, she worked to help children who were forced to fight as soldiers and with women in villages who had seen and survived horrible violence.

Leymah realised how important women could be in restoring and keeping peace in her country, saying 'If any changes were to be made in society, it had to be by the mothers.'

A second civil war started only three years later, and Leymah became more and more influential as a peace activist. She co-founded a peacebuilding network for women to work together across West Africa, and led a peace group bringing together Christian and Muslim women in Liberia. Neither of these things had ever been done before.

Leymah inspired thousands of women all over the country to come and join the peace movement in the capital city. They gathered in the streets and markets in huge numbers, praying for peace and staging daily non-violent protests. This was very dangerous as the president had forbidden it and he often killed people who went against him.

When nothing seemed to be happening at official peace talks, Leymah led hundreds of women to sit in protest on the floor outside the room, blocking the politicians from leaving and putting pressure on them to agree peace.

Her efforts helped to bring peace just weeks later and to elect the country's first female president in another two years' time. Leymah won the Nobel Peace Prize in 2011 and continues to work internationally for peace and women's rights. She gives talks around the world to promote peaceful, progressive causes and inspire a new generation of activists.

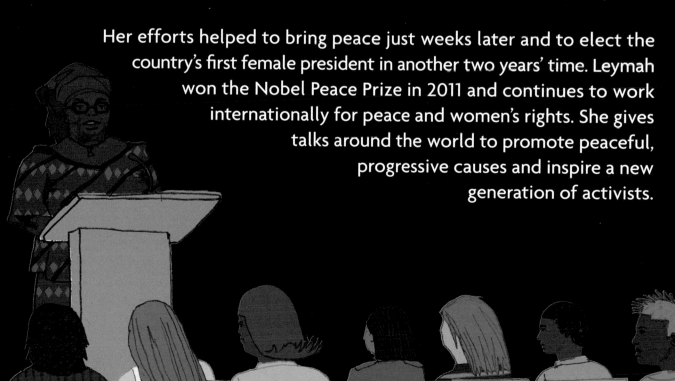

Activate! Draw a Peace Path

Peace and conflict can seem like such big and complicated ideas that it's hard to know where to start doing your bit to help create a more peaceful world. But there are lots of things that you can do, and your actions can also inspire others to live more peacefully.

Why not create a Peace Path? It can help you and your friends or classmates learn to resolve arguments peacefully.

How it works

A Peace Path works best with two people at a time. Both people walk together along the Peace Path, one step at a time, and take it in turns to follow the prompts written on each step.

By listening respectfully and expressing their frustrations calmly and clearly, they should find a solution that works for everyone by the end of the path.

SHAKE HANDS

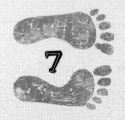

9   Thank you.

7   You can ...

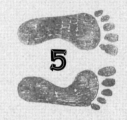

5   Thank you.

From now on I will ...

3   I know that you feel ... when ...

How can i make it right?

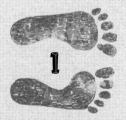

1   I feel ... when ...

ORANGE SIDE GOES FIRST

START HERE

26

LEAVE IN PEACE

Challenge

Ask if you can draw a Peace Path somewhere on the ground with chalk or paint. If you can paint it on the ground that is best, as it means lots of children will have the chance to use it over time.

If you aren't allowed to draw on the ground, then draw a path on big sheets of paper or cardboard and stick them to the ground for this activity.

Thank you.

From now on
I will ...

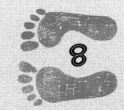

Thank you.

How can I
make it right?

You can ...

Use the example Peace Path on these pages as a starting point, and talk with your friends or classmates about whether you want to change or add any steps – maybe you could vote on it.

I know that you
feel ... when ...

I feel ... when ...

Come up with fun, colourful designs for each step along the path – make sure to remember that the footprints show both people where to stand!

START HERE

Organise!
A day of peace

Hold a day of peace to help your friends better understand what peace is, how people are affected by conflict and how we can resolve conflicts peacefully.

Ask volunteers to work in groups to organise different activities that people can watch or take part in on the day. You could come up with your own ideas and ask people to suggest their own, too. Here are a few activity ideas to get you started.

win-win debate

A traditional debate has a winner and a loser, depending on who argued their point of view best.

In a win-win debate, however, the focus is on who comes up with the best solutions for resolving a disagreement and behaves in a respectful way towards their 'opponent'. Points are taken away for any angry or disrespectful behaviour.

Co-operative games

Search online for different co-operative games, where you have to work together to succeed.

Try Balloon Bounce. Stand in a circle holding hands and work together to keep a balloon in the air. You can't use your feet or let go of each other's hands.

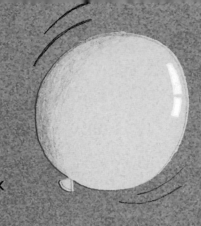

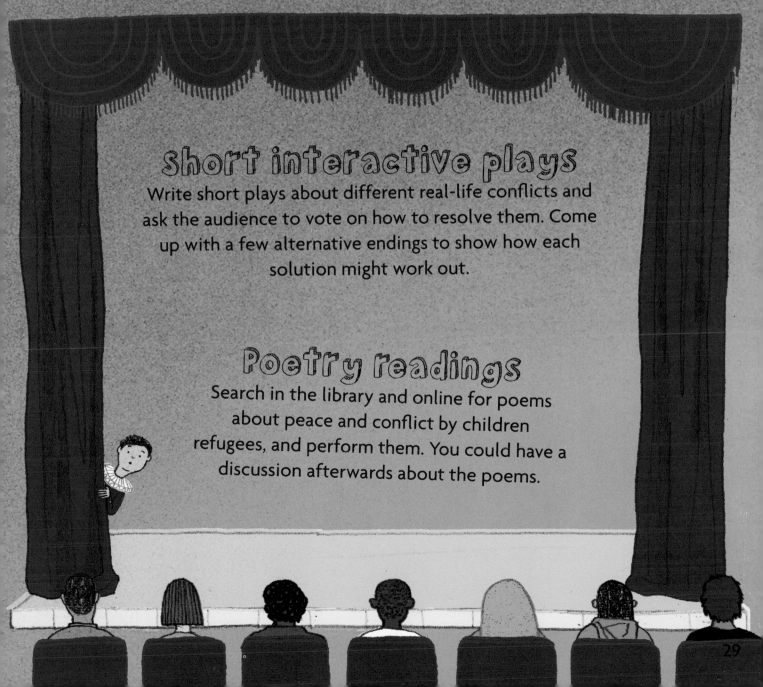

short interactive plays

Write short plays about different real-life conflicts and ask the audience to vote on how to resolve them. Come up with a few alternative endings to show how each solution might work out.

Poetry readings

Search in the library and online for poems about peace and conflict by children refugees, and perform them. You could have a discussion afterwards about the poems.

Glossary

armed violence hurting or killing people with weapons, such as guns or bombs

civil war a war between different groups in the same country

compromise a type of agreement in which people who want different things decide to each give up or change part of what they want in order to stop the argument

conflict any kind of tense or angry disagreement, from a difference of opinion to full-scale war

ethnicity describes being a member of a group that shares the same culture, language, racial identity or history

gender how a person sees their identity as a woman or a man, or both or neither – it doesn't always match up with the sex (girl, boy or intersex) they were given at birth

mediate to help people work through their conflict by leading talks between them and keeping things calm

negotiate to come to an agreement with someone, or help others to do the same

rebels people who fight against, or are not loyal to, the government of their country

refugee a person forced to leave their country to escape danger and find safety in another place

sanctions punishments that don't use violence, such as banning trade with a country, that aim to change that country's actions

Sanskrit an ancient language of India

sexual orientation describes someone's feelings of attraction, whether that is to women, men or non-binary people (those who don't feel they are entirely woman or man)

terrorism the threat or use of violence, especially against civilians (people not in the armed forces), linked to a political or religious view

trauma an emotional shock that can have a serious, long-lasting effect on someone's mind and body

United Nations an organisation with many member countries that works for world peace and development

Further information

Children in our World: Global Conflict
Louise Spilsbury (Wayland, 2016)
In this book you can learn about the issues and conflicts that are going on today around the world. Discover more about how war and conflict affect people and what you can do to help them.

Politics for Beginners
Louie Stowell (Usborne, 2018)
This book is a clear illustrated guide to the big issues that affect people's everyday lives all over the world. Learn about the different ways governments work, see how conflict can develop within and between countries and get tips on how to debate difficult issues positively.

Why Do We Fight?: Conflict, War and Peace
Niki Walker (Franklin Watts, 2014)
Learn more about how small disagreements can grow into bigger and more serious ones, and how world conflicts compare with those in your own everyday life. Understand more about why we fight and, most importantly, what we can do to avoid it.

Websites

youtube.com/watch?v=IToa1OMIOe8&t=6s
A short but helpful video with five top tips to resolve an argument peacefully.

youtube.com/watch?v=o0bB75pAZ0w
Muzoon, a young woman from Syria, tells us about her hopes for an end to the war that meant she had to leave her home country.

youtube.com/watch?v=rwN2R5zd0bw
A photo slideshow of twelve different places around the world before and after war.

youtube.com/watch?v=QoIafzc0k74
A short video explaining a bit more about what the United Nations is and how it works for world peace and development.

Note to parents and teachers: every effort has been made by the Publishers to ensure websites are suitable for children, that they are of the highest educational value, and that they contain no inappropriate or offensive material. However, because of the nature of the Internet, it is impossible to guarantee that the contents of these sites will not be altered. We strongly advise that Internet access is supervised by a responsible adult.

Index